Contents

I DON'T GIVE A D*MN!

I Don't Give a D*MN!

A Self-Motivation Guide To Living Free

AVONDA ANDERSON

Melanated Rich, Inc

I AM a proud Queen Mother, Mother, Daughter, Sister, Aunt, Cousin, Niece, and Friend.

Because of you, I AM!

First Printing, 2022
Publisher: Melanated Rich, Inc

About This Book

Your mind is like a tree. The branches are the thoughts that grow from your mind. The leaves or fruit it produces are your desires. You can grow good and bad leaves or fruit, depending on what nutrients or the type of thinking you are supplying each branch of thought. If you are constantly thinking negative thoughts or responding negatively to situations, then you are going to get negative results. Or if you think positively, you will get positive results. Your mind can only produce what you think about yourself and the world around you. Knowing this, will allow you to always ensure your mind is working in harmony with your desired outcome.

This guidebook will aid you through the four stages in the process, to reach the *I Don't Give A D*MN!* mind-set. At this level of awareness, you are ready to conquer your greatest fears and achieve your wildest dreams. You are your own imagination in action, and you are the creator of your own reality. When you truly know this and are ready to put this knowledge to practice your life will never be the same. Here, you will not care about the opinions of others or be swayed by things out of your control. You will know that you create your own circumstances. And, to all negative information, people, places, and things you will say *I DON'T GIVE A D*MN* and move forward anyway. Here, your mind will be free to elevate to the highest levels of *I Don't Give A D*MN!* in all its glory. It is all up to you to put this guide to practice. If you will think about it, you will be about it! And that, it. Can be whatever your imagination can conceive, that you can believe. You must motivate yourself to do it.

Motivation is what keeps you going. It is the reason people succeed and the reason people fail. Motivation is the drive someone must have to complete any task. The ingredients of motivation are combined with many factors which include your attitude, the people you hang around, the way you think, knowing yourself, helping other people and so much more.

The purpose of this guidebook is to take you through methods you can practice daily to remain motivated to reaching your goals. These techniques can help you feel better about yourself in everything you do. You can take these methods with you when you go to work and when you are at home. Motivation is the spark everyone needs to make it throughout the day, to set and meet goals, and more. Without motivation you will fail. When you have apathy toward something. You are not motivated because you could not care either way. This is the worst attitude you can have. Someone who feels this way is not capable of achieving anything because they do not care if they do or not. If you are feeling this way. This guidebook is exactly what you need to help you overcome your negative attitude and begin feeling positive and motivated again. When you know how to remain motivated with yourself you can also help others because your attitude will be contagious. When you practice daily motivational techniques eventually, they will come to you naturally. At first these methods may be different for you to do or to remember that what you are use to. It will take time for you to begin to naturally practice and follow these techniques.

Self-Evaluation

10 Questions you should ask yourself: A preparation for self-improvement.

Are you ready to be all you can be? Or are you content with your life the way things are? Do you aspire for something deeper and more meaningful in your life?

Below are ten questions you should ask yourself to prepare you to get motivated to living free. Take a moment after and reflect on the things you write down. These will be the basis to determine your areas of self-improvement before you can reach the *I Don't Give A D*MN!* mindset.

1. What do I really want?

The question of the ages. So many things you want to do with your life and so little time or money to do them, right? Are you ready to get what you want by doing the things required to have it? Are you willing to stand alone and wait for the right time get it?

Write what you think you want and what you think you can have?

2. Should I really change?

What does redefining 'self', look like for you? Would it change your lifestyle for the better? What about your personality, that you do not like when interacting with others?

Write how will you change yourself and what you will change below:

3. What's the bright side in all of this?

With so much happening around you there seems to be no room for even considering that light at the end of the tunnel. But can you see it? Are you hopeful? Do you have joy in your life? Do you always prepare for the worst, or do you see the sliver lining in the sky?

Write what you are positive about below: Begin each sentence with I AM.

4. Am I comfortable with what I am doing?

Do you find joy in the things you do? Or are you always stressed and agitated. Are you willing to be extremely uncomfortable for a short while to achieve maximum comfort long term? Does your current job or business energize you or drain you?

Write what and how you are comfortable with what you are doing below: Begin each sentence with I AM.

5. Have I done enough for myself?

Have you done all that you can for yourself? Or is there something more you want to do? Discontentment in every aspect can be dangerous in large doses, but in tiny amounts you will be able to see and do stuff you could never imagine doing. Do you take time for personal care? Do you do for others more than you do for yourself?

Write what you have done for yourself and what else you want to do for you below:

6. Am I happy at where I am today?

Are you happy where you are today? Or do you struggle with depression and anxiety? Do the people around make you feel happy about being around them? Do you feel happy as yourself when you are around them? Are you happy with your job? The city you live in?

Write what you are happy about below: Begin each sentence with I AM.

7. Do I have an appealing personality?

Do people like being around you. Are you easy going? Or are you constantly fussing with someone or about something? Do you say good morning back to someone who says it to you first? Are you laid back or always ready to fight? Do you say excuse me, please and thank you more than it's said to you in reply or in return?

Write how appealing you think your personality is:

8. How much money could I have?

How much are you willing to work for it? How much are you willing to let go for it? How would having money make you feel when you have it? How would you use money for yourself?

Write how much money you thank you could have and what you could have with it below:

9. What motivates me?

What motivates you? It is an answer you have to find out for yourself. What and who are the people, places, and things that make you feel happy?

Write what motivates you below:

10. Who AM I Really?

Do you know who you really are? Are you ready to be what you always wanted to be? Who do you think you are?

Write who you are below: Begin each sentence with I AM.

Chapter One

Think It: Define Your Desire

Only You Can Decide What You Want To Have Or To Do

For most, deciding what to do is the hardest thing to do. It requires commitment to the unknown and the uncertainty of the unknown can be too overwhelming to overcome at times. That uncertainty, at times, is so overwhelming that other people become uncertain for you, don't they? There you are, minding your defining desire business, getting your dreams all laid out how you want them, almost reaching the heights of *I Don't Give A D*MN!* mindset, and **BAM!** @#$, here they come the dream killers. The faith stealers, the negative know it all, the naysayers, the unbelievers, the imagination smash-ers, you know them, HATERS! Here they come, trying to tell you what is not possible and why they do not think this will do this or that. All the while now, you start to catch their fear and then you try to find loopholes in your dreams to fit the fear described. You start saying what if this, if that and before you know it, there goes your dreams unfulfilled. Now you are miserable back on the *"Lord why not me train "* or the *"It will happen on God's time cruise ship "*, back unhappy with them.

Are you not tired of this cycle yet? I know I was tired of being in that constant loop of developing nega-tive thoughts and emotions. I got tired of letting other people's opinions take my attention away from the goals I set for myself. It was not until I focused, in my mind, on what it was that I was really trying to achieve. That I started to see the specific expressions of things that I desired. Showing up in the specific ways in which I wanted them to happen. From this I have learned that deciding is the easy part, sticking with the decision de-spite its popularity or understanding by anyone, place, or thing outside of yourself is the not so easy part. But if you do, stay focused on the things you desire and not let outside influences distract you. You can have what you want, you can be who you want, and you can do what you want to do. There is only one economy I believe in and that is the economy of thought! You can appropriate anything into your physical attainment, if you can think of it in your mind's imagination, first!

Living Free Starts In The Mind First

The question is, are you ready? Are you ready to free your mind from limitations and lack? Are you ready to acknowledge that your world is the image of the thoughts you subject yourself to thinking? Are you ready to think positively, consciously, and deliberately about yourself and others? If you said yes to being ready, right here and now, decide your desire. Decide to have the life or job, business, love, money that you want. Desires are simply positive thoughts of yourself and others.

Yes, you can even desire on the behalf of others. Truth be told, that is the best gift you can ever give someone. Seeing them in your mind, giving agreement to them having and being who they want to be. Just make sure you desire on their behalf positively. Because Karma is a wish granter, she will grant onto you whatever thought you have for another.

So, make sure you only wish for loving things. Even for those that do not love you. You have been warned of this with what is known as the golden rule. Do unto others as you want them done unto you.

Think Before You Act, That Is A Fact

We spend so much time reacting and doing things that we do not think, most of the time. You know this is true because how many times have you said or heard; *What were you thinking*? Remember, your mind and the ability to think is the most powerful gift your creator bestowed upon you. It is the only thing you have complete and absolute control over. And this guide will show you exactly how to take control of your mind and direct it to define the purpose in your life of your own choosing.

When you have control of your mind, you reap the benefits of all the good you desire such as good health, money, joy, peace of mind and freedom from worry and fear. When you do not take control of your mind and define your purpose, someone else will do it for you and you may find yourself in poverty, ill health, envious and jealous of others. But with practice you will prepare your mind to only see yourself as you desire.

As you go through life you will find there are certain circumstances that you have absolutely no control of. I know you find yourself asking who would choose an unpleasant experience for themselves. Or you are saying, I did not ask for my life to be this way. But as you know, most things through life are out of your control. However, your positive attitude will help you manage your life and the things you do. I know how hard it is to fathom, but the truth is. Your life is what you make it now. You can change your circumstance, you can get out of depression, despair, and worry. You can get out of poverty, and you can have the big house if you want it. But can you see it for yourself? Do you even think you deserve it? I am here to tell you that you deserve it and if you use this guidebook, you will be able to think good things for yourself, and your life will change as you see it in your mind.

Your Imagination Is The Center Of Your Reality

Your mind is always in a state of creation whether you are aware of it or not. Your outer world is a mirror image of what you think about. If you desire and think of abundance, you will have it. If you think of lack and limitation, you will create it. That is why thinking of your desire is the first stage of the process to living free. You can only achieve what your mind can conceive.

This principle is the basis for all creations, it starts in the mind first. It does not matter of any social or educational status either. Anyone can do this, and anyone can achieve any level of success they can think of for themselves. Only you know where you would like to be in the future.

One thing to note is that during this stage your only concern is to think of your desire. Do not be concerned with the how. Even if you have failed in the past, keep thinking positive and focus your mind on the desired outcome. And if you can stay in the assumption of having what you want even before it is visible to you. Trust me, when I tell you the universal energy will align everything and everyone for your desire to come to life.

Prepare Your Mind & Visualize It

Now that you know what you want. The next step in defining your desire, is to see it in your mind. It is time to use your imagination and begin to visualize it. What is visualization? In this guide, visualization is defined as the formation of mental visual images. Below are steps you must take to prepare your mind for the imagination to form mental visual images.

Once you can **think of** your desire and **visualize from** it. You are well on your way to stage two, of the process which you will learn in the next chapter. Where you will be guided through how to use your decisions to get off *Fear Alley Way* and go all the way up to the corner of, *I Don't Give A D*MN! Blvd.* and *I Create My Own Reality Mindset Ave.*

How to Mentally Visualize

Visualize at night right before you go to sleep (10 to 20 mins), so that your desire is established in your subconscious while you sleep. Bringing your desire ever closer to you.

1. Find a quiet space

2. Get comfortable *(lie down)*

3. Close your eyes to the senses *(smell, touch, taste, hearing, sight)*

4. Open your mind's eye to the sense of feeling and see the thing, place, or person in your imagination.

5. Be specific of exactly what you want to have, do, go or be

6. Give the image sensory feeling by seeing it with all the expressions and vividness as if it were real. (*Stay here for as long as you can stay focused on the assumption that the desire is real without you having physical possession of it*).

7. Open your eyes and remain in the feeling with gratitude for the ability to use this power for your good.

8. Repeat this daily for 7 days up to 30 days until the desire manifests. (*The key here is to be alert so you will recognize your desire as you visualized) If it still has not come, then wait for it and keep practicing these steps as an act of faith in the thing desired)*

Chapter Two

Write It: Physical Confirmation

Turn Your Words Into Action

In the previous chapter you learned the power you have in the thoughts you think. Now that you have decided what you want, have a clear understanding of exactly what you want, and you can visualize it in your mind. The next step in the process is to write it down.

Writing your desire down helps to start the process of raising your belief and faith energies. Writing down your goals is the first actionable step you take in attaining your stated desire. It is the first physical confirmation of the desire you wish to manifest.

For example, if you want a car. You must write down what type of car, the make the model, the color of the inside and outside, the interior (cloth or leather), etc. You must write down every detail as you visualize it.

When writing your desire, it should clearly state exactly what it is that you want. Notice, I did not say need. Because the thought of need, creates an awareness of lack. And because as you think, so you are. You must always remember to think from the abundance of want. It should be as you have visualized it

Your Written Word Is Your Bond

Having the word written down, creates a powerful energy of creation. As you start to motivate yourself and start believing and having faith in the wish unfulfilled. You begin to move closer to alignment with it. You begin to shift your thinking to a state of gratitude, happiness and joy for the blessings already given to you. You believe that you deserve the things and life you want to have, even when you have not materialized it yet.

Writing down your desire helps you also elevate the physical senses to expect the desire you want to come into your existence of awareness. You begin to see the thing you desire all around you. I can attest to this because it happened to me. When I used this method to manifest my first beauty supply store, that I opened in St. Louis, MO in 2017, called Melanated Rich, now online at www.melantedrich.com. Where I sold organic hair, cosmetics, and skin care products. I remember visualizing the store even before I wrote the business plan or had any products to sell. Following this process, I first had the thought. Then, I saw and felt its realness in my mind. After that, I wrote it down. The point I want you to take away is that. Opening that store was something that I had a desire to do, and I did it. That desire was fulfilled, because only I can define my level of success achieved. And only you can define yours for you.

Since then, I have fulfilled other desires all by following the process in this guidebook. However, I must warn you to be mindful during this stage of the process. During this stage it is important to keep visualizing and having positive thoughts and do not give up on your idea the moment things do not go as you planned. Because even while doing these things. It took a span of a year to manifest into my physical possession of it. That is because I had to pay the price of cleaning up my credit and raising capital. Writing a plan and setting my budget. Going out testing products and finding vendors. I had to be patient and trust the process of birth. Just as it takes a baby months to be born. Your desires or ideas need time to develop and germinate. In other words, once your desire is planted in the mind, keep feeding it belief and faith and then wait for it to grow and develop, into your wish being fulfilled. Soon it will be born or manifested into your physical possession of it. I can assure you, that it will always come at the right time, and it is never late.

The important thing to note here is that any desire starts in the mind and then it must be written down for you to gain awareness of it in your physical senses.

Only What You Believe Is What You Can Achieve

To have faith in something means you begin to expect it. In other words, your thoughts are as you expect. So, expect only the good things. And more good things will start to happen for you. On the other hand, if you expect the worst to happen, the worst will happen. This is the law of the universe; you attract what you think you will. So, take your written desire and begin to expect it. This is not an exercise or demonstration of physical will, but a mental one.

Writing your desire down, mentality prepares your mind for your good. You are acting as if you are expecting it and you start to believe in the desire and have faith it will come into your physical possession. And trust me, it will blossom and will come just at the right time and if it is coming late, then wait! Because your only job is to desire (ask and it shall be given to you), the universal energy will align the means of the how. As its ways are past finding out. Because all things are possible and if you can believe it, you will achieve it according to your faith, be it unto you. Writing down your desire is you believing enough of your desire to act on making it real by writing it down.it gives you a constant reminder of the things you would want to accomplish. It will get to a place in your mind, that you cannot see why you cannot do anything you put your mind to.

Written Word
Precedes Physical Signs

Now when it comes to writing your desire. First, it must be clear and state exactly what you want. Do speak plainly here, be exact. You should have a clear image in your mind by now of the desired outcome. For instance, if you are sick, your desire is to be healthy. So, your statement would be something like. I see myself in good health or I desire good health. Second, you must state what you will give to obtain it.

Because, you know that you cannot get something for nothing. You must be willing to give what it takes for your desire to come to fruition. For instance, good health requires a proper diet and exercise. So, your giving statement could be something like; In exchange for good health, I will exercise three times per week, go meatless two days a week and eat more vegetables. You must invest or give these things in exchange for good health, would you not agree? Same thing if you have a desire to be rich, you must be willing to invest in being rich by understanding economics, financial planning, investing, etc. This is the part of the equation that most people miss and fail to attain the things they genuinely want. Now, the question is, what price are you willing to pay to have what you want?

You Must Give Into Yourself To Receive From Yourself

Remember, to always be in an awareness state of gratitude asking the universal energy to give you the wisdom you need to control your own mind and use it wisely toward whatever desired outcome you want. If you do these two things as suggested. You will start to see your world reflect the things you have created in your mind. Whatever, your desire is, start from this moment in giving what it is you need to give to get it.

To give (time, attention, and energy), it must be given with love and a good positive mental attitude. Be happy and rejoice because your desire is near. In fact, it is already given to you the moment you ask for it or desire it. Now you just must align yourself with it. How do you align yourself with it? By keeping your thoughts positive and believing that what you desire is what you deserve.

What do you deserve then? Only you can know this and only you can define what it means for you. You deserve as much as you think you do and that is what you will get. When you know what you deserve, you know your worth. And this will help you to know when a situation, place, person, or thing is not of value to you. So, set your own standards, because if you do not others will do it for you. Putting this guidebook into practice will ensure you get exactly what you think you deserve your desire to be.

Write Your Own Desire

Use the temple on the next page to write your desire and the price you are willing to pay to get it. Write your clearly defined desire here, repeat throughout the day every day until memorized.

Desire Statement: (what you want)

-
-
-
-
-

Giving Statement: (price of want)

-
-
-
-
-
-

Chapter Three

Speak It: Mind Motivating Method

Life's Happening Through You, Not To You

Now that you have decided what you want, and you have written it down. It is time to act, but as stated above, this action is not any outwardly physical acts. This acting is taking place all in your mind, in your imagination. You cannot attain any physical manifestation unless you first get it in your mind. Everything that was made and being made started as a thought and that active thought persisted, and the universal energy aligned and turned those thoughts into physical things.

This mental action is called the Mind Motivating Method: do this in the morning upon waking if possible and again right before you sleep. Continuous practice is extremely important to motivation. Every day you should maintain a routine of practicing these techniques.

First: You want to repeat your written desire for at least 10 to 15 times in your mind only, do this until you have your goal memorized. Doing this will impress upon your mind's imagination to act and create a vivid picture of your desire until it feels as real as the physical possession of it. It will also help build up positive thoughts and elevate your energies of faith and belief. Making it harder for your own negative thoughts and others to impose their negative thoughts on you. The opinions of the world will have no effect on you. You will no longer be moved by the opinions of the world. Bringing you closer to reaching *I Don't Give A D*MN!* levels.

The **second:** step of the Mind Motivating Method is to start saying your desire aloud to yourself only. You should be able to verbalize your written desire by heart. You should have memorized it first, as suggested in this guide to do so first.

Speak it to believe it

When you speak your desires aloud to yourself, you are activating your belief energy consciously. You must believe in your desire fully yourself before you share it with others. Even when people discourage you and tell you that you are wasting your time. Speaking it will give you the strength to stand firm in your belief. By doing this, you will have gone a long way to pay the price in obtaining your desire. Which is simply the effort you intend to give in following this guide as given you.

Speaking your desire as you see it, will bring you closer to moving to the *I Don't Give A D*MN* mindset. You will get in the habit of believing in yourself and in your abilities of your own choosing. The things you desire will be earned with your own merit and on your own accord. You will not let anyone, or anything stop you from pursuing your goals, so long as it does not take or cause harm to another in its pursuit.

Speaking takes the written word and breaths live into them. So that it soon materializes into physical posses-sion. Knowing this, be mindful of the words you speak of yourself and others or the words you allow others to speak on to you. That is why you are warned; let your yes mean yes and your no mean no. Because you cannot say one thing and expect another. If you are speaking negatively about yourself or others, you cannot expect to receive results that are favorable to you. Negativity can be infectious in situations. You want to be sure the people you are talking to are positive. If the person you choose to hang out with is a negative person who is always complaining and who sees the negative side of everything, they might not be who you want to help you become motivated. Negativity will only bring you down and cause you to be negative too. The experience you receive will be as you speak of it. Consequently, it is extremely important to choose your words wisely and say what you mean and mean what you say.

When your negative traits come up, do not recognize them. Do not give them any recognition of mind or speech. Stop putting yourself down and stop letting others put you down. What you speak, is what you energize. Make sure you discredit and correct what you do not like. Instead, confirm and exclaim the good you do like. Focus on your strengths. When you focus on things you are good at it makes you feel good. When you focus on your strengths and things you enjoy. You will become motivated to achieve goals focused on these things.

If two or more agree, it shall be

To accelerate your desired manifestation, you can take the extra step and form a motivating mastermind with one or more people that you can work in harmony with to attain your desire as you have defined it. Therefore, you must choose only those who are going to speak positively towards you.

It is important to note that if you cannot have a cheerful outlook in your current city of residence or job of employment. Then move to a new city or get a new job that will allow you to elevate your mind to positive thinking and be around positive people. The things around you have a great deal to do with the way you feel and if you will be motivated or stuck in a funk. Forming a motivating mastermind, means keeping good company and hanging out with others who are supportive of you and your goals for life. You want to be around people who support you and believe in you too. For example, if you have goals to be a successful entrepreneur with your own business. You should spend time together with people who are supportive. If you are around people who are negative about your endeavors and unsupportive you will not feel good about it at all. Cut the negativity out. If these people are family members, it could be the most difficult decision you ever make. However, it will be the best thing you can do for you. If people are not support-ive or positive, then cut them out.

Mentorship and coaching are positive forms of creat-ing masterminds and I encourage you to invest in them. This guidebook is a great tool to use to find mastermind alliances. To get ahead in your life, I am here to tell you that you do not need to waste time for no reason. Because the totally unique ideas out there have already been done. And the ideas that are out there now, are just reiterations of others. You might know this as a remake, like a remake of a song,

For most things, there is already a blueprint for you to follow and make your own. This is the secret that most elite people, as they are called, use to accelerate their place in life. They master the use and skills of others to promote themselves to higher levels of life. And you can do it too. Are you ready to remake your life's song? Re-member, what is meant for you, is for you.

The only one able to block your blessing is you.

The attitude is the gardener of your life's garden

Ready to evaluate it? To do so, start right now and begin to have a positive attitude with everyone you encounter through the day. Only listen to good things and only hear and speak words of good. Do this for two weeks and you will start to notice a positive change in the atmosphere when people are around you. Please note that, you do not need to announce you are giving positive vibes, just do it naturally and watch what happens. You will be so much happier, and others will be willing to aid you ensuring you achieve your goals. It really is just that simple. Keep doing this to keep planting good seeds in your garden to bear the sweetest and juiciest fruit for you to enjoy in abundance.

Now that you have learned of the first three steps to having the life you want: *Think It-->Write It-->Speak It.* In the next chapter, you will learn the last and ultimate step in the process of achieving the *I Don't Give A D*MN!* mindset.

It is a form of power that does not recognize the word impossible. When you master it, you will obtain anything you want so easily; it will seem that life is your personal magic show.

Chapter Four

Feel it: Faith Brings the Blessing to Life

Elevate Your Awareness, Shut Your Mind From The Senses

The subject in this step is your greatest asset because it is the means for you to tap into the universal power of creation itself. You can use it for the attainment of anything you desire. Earlier in this guide, you learned that the only thing you have complete control over is your mind. Well, before you can take control of your mind, you must believe or have faith that you can do so. Faith is the proof of things not seen. Faith is your thought in action, the expression of things hoped for. When you apply faith to a desire it enables you to consciously become the thing you desire. Faith is belief expressed as feeling. Faith causes the unseen desire to be seen and experienced by the physical senses.

I remember when I just returned to the US, from living aboard in Malaysia, heartbroken and not having anything. I mean, I had nothing. No job, no home of my own, no car, no money! It was in this state of despair that I found my faith. and I discovered just how powerful I was. Right from there I started to study and meditate and visualize the life that I wanted.

From that time forward, I have overcome challenges due to my belief I was deserving of all that I could see myself being, having and doing. I stayed faithful to this and now I am doing everything that I want to do. I have everything that I want and more. I did it by following the methods and motivations in this guide. And you can do it now, too. The question is though, will you? Will you have faith in yourself when no one else believes in you? Can you keep your faith, in the face of a challenge to what you believe to be true? Faith is the prerequisite for receiving any blessing.

Faith Seals The Deal

Applying faith is the means in which you take this control and what motivates you in achieving the things you desire. Like anything there are positives and negatives to faith. You can have faith in the undesirable things (poverty, ill health, social injustice) and you can see from the world around you that most people are applying faith negatively in this way. Most people in the world have failed to take control of their own mind and use it to obtain what they want. They have for an instance lost all hope (belief) in themselves. And in doing so they limit themselves to the conditions they can only sense. They no longer believe in their imagination. They no longer believe all things are possible to the one that believes and has faith in that, in which they desire.

What most fail to realize is that, even if they are not consciously aware of it or not, they are still creating. Then, what are you creating? Look at your world, and test how well you are controlling your attitude, applying faith and belief positively to change your circumstance. I have been in a few situations that I was able to immediately impact by changing my mind and having faith in the desired change. Instead of looking to the outside, I tune my energy inward. I sat with myself and visualized the outcome I desired and in a brief time things changed for my good. Faith is required first, before you can get the blessing. You must apply faith correctly before you can ever physically take possession of your desire.

Again, do not be moved by the circumstances outside of your control. You must have faith in the possibility of good even despite what appears to be going wrong. Faith will cause the agreement between the thought of something and appropriation of something to you for your benefit. Like the old saying goes, faith without works is dead. If you do not apply faith actively in your mind positively towards what you want. Then your desire will remain dead or unfulfilled.

Remember faith is, belief expressed as feeling. In other words, you must feel that you are blessed to be blessed. You must feel happy to be happy. You must feel successful to be successful. Faith seals the feeling to the belief in the attainment of your desire. Accordingly, be faithful. And what you want, will obey to it.

Faith Gets The Blessings

Of course, it is easy to believe and have faith in the things you can see, feel, and touch. However, it is another thing to have faith and belief in the unseen. This is when faith counts the most, when you can apply it positively to the desire you have yet to see with the senses of the physical eye. You have no idea how it is going to happen, but you know that it will happen. And so, you believe in your mind that you have it already. When you have applied faith correctly, you begin to feel that the desire is real, even before you take physical possession of it.

This is faith in action or feeling. Feeling is the emotional state that results from positively applying faith. Feeling is what allows you to keep going in the face of defeat, it is the beginning of grounding your desires into their physical attainment.

People are often not successful because they lack the confidence to believe and have faith that they can have what they want. Procrastination is a result of this lack of confidence to believe. The effects can also be damaging if your procrastination causes problems with your work life, personal life and more. Putting things off is a fundamental problem for a vast number of people. Many people are very aware they procrastinate but they cannot get out of the funk they are stuck in. You can. It is common to sit around and think about how things could be or how things will be. Instead of them doing anything about it, they have permanent residency on Fear Ally Way and do not know why they cannot seem to get out of worry and misery. Most have lost their faith and belief and without these, you cannot elevate to the feeling of hope. Failure is the result of the lack of belief in self. To be successful you must increase your capacity of belief in yourself. Once you do this, you can command anything you want out of life.

Let Your Prayers Always Be In Harmony

Did you notice that I said command and not beg for the things you want? The universal energy never intended for you to beg for anything. This would imply that a force, on the outside of your mind is responsible for the outcome in your life. But if you have been following this guide you know that your outcomes in life are controlled 100% by you. And You were born to be great, and it should be your only purpose in life to achieve that greatness whatever it may be for you.

To increase the capacity of belief in yourself, your prayers must be in harmony with what you want. You must pray or meditate with positive intention even when you are not feeling positive yet. The persistent thought of being positive will strengthen your belief in it, even when you are not feeling positive about it yet. Keep praying positive good things and your belief will deepen as you persist in thinking about it. Be careful here because you can have belief in negative things too. And because you already know that what you reap is what you sow. Always, be mindful of only sowing good to reap. If you are not where you want to be or doing what you want to do or having what you want to have, then change it. Follow the steps as suggested in this guide, as I have, and you are well on your way to achieving the life you desire. You can do this by keeping your mind focused only on the things you want and not the things you do not want. As your mind knows no difference, it just produces the thoughts desired.

The Only Limits On You Are The Ones You Imply

I would know because I was once held back by thoughts of limitations. For a long time, I imposed on myself limitations such as fear(worry), anger and poverty. I blamed others and the system for it not being fair. I used to worry how I was going to buy food and pay bills. I used to be angry and depressed about not getting a promotion at work and not making the money I wanted. Even through all these challenges, I always believed in myself. I knew I deserved better than what I was currently experiencing at the time. And instead of sitting in my pity, I started to do some research and started to read positive books such as Think and Grow Rich by Napoleon Hill and Freedom for All by Neville Goddard.

Reading these books and lectures available online, helped me to cultivate a new mind of positive thinking. With the understanding bestowed upon me from their teachings and methods. I started to take complete control of what I thought and what I let others think for and of me. I cut off negative people and negative habits that were keeping me from reaching my goals. I begin to understand that the entire world is made up of one energy. Now I know that all things have a frequency to and from that energy. Just like with an antenna if you do not tune to the right frequency or station, you will not get the right message broadcasting. It is the same for your blessing.

Your blessing of desires has a frequency you must tune into to receive the signal or the blessing. To do this, you must control your mind to think positive so that you are broadcasting a vibrational message that matches the commanded desire. Everything you want is within your reach. You must believe you are limitless to be limitless. And if I could overcome my challenges, I know you can do it too.

Your thoughts and actions will determine how far and fast you get in your life as you want it. The point here is to always control how you respond to negative situations, places, and things. You can only control how you respond. Never argue with people because your truth does not need validation from their ignorance. Because it is your truth and yours alone. Remember that your blessings only require YOU needing to believe and have faith in it, for you to achieve it. You just simply need to choose. Choose what you want to believe in and choose to believe in the choices you choose.

Things Happen As You Perceive Them

Remember, faith is only limited by what you believe you can achieve. Your life reflects how you have applied faith in it. Accept defeat as a challenge to keep going and keep your faith.

Below are **three key** practice takeaways to feeling your way to the blessing.

1. Know what you want and believe that you can get it. Even before you take physical possession of it.
2. You must see it clearly in your mind first! Remember, you must think about it to achieve it.
3. Pay attention to your intuition, trust your gut. Something I have learned to do after I have failed many times when I did not do so. It will warn you when you are off track of your goal and will give you insights when you are on track. And when you feel inspired to, act at once.

Feeling to the Blessing Formula

(**Define** it + Believe in It)*Positive Attitude
=Faith Applied

Faith Applied * Positive Attitude = Feeling to
the Blessing

Chapter Five

No Empty Hands Please

What are empty hands and how can you avoid them? Well, empty hands are any negative thoughts (yours or others); they are the people you help who can never help you; it is the feelings of doubt and worry or other negative emotions of low vibrating frequency; it is jobs with no advancement; it is state and federal taxes; it is dating emotionally challenged individuals. It is anything that drains your energy, time, and money. You want to stay away and say no to these empty-handed situations, people, places, and things.

And on the other side, you can also have full handed situations. Full hands are positive thoughts, positive people that support you and pour into you; it is getting that promotion or new job offer; it is having confidence in yourself; it is finding love in yourself you can share with someone. It is anything that makes you feel good about doing, being and having what you want.

Having full hands at all times is the highest achievement of *I Don't Give A D*MN!* To reach the *I Don't Give A D*MN!* mindset, you will transcend past the need to look for answers to any of your problems, on the outside of your own mind. You are feeling ok where you are and where you are is feeling ok. All things are always happening for your good. Even the things you think are against you, will be working for your good. When you reach the, *I Don't Give A D*MN!* mindset, you will not have the energy to care what other people are thinking or doing. Because you will be too busy motivating your mind to prepare it for all the good you desire.

Focus on that, and watch your world change right in front of your eyes. You are as limited as your mind will allow. You are as free as you think you are. You will not need to take from anyone, and you will not look for anyone to give you. You will use your imagination to create at will. Using this guide and the below affirmations and visualization techniques will aid you as you navigate the higher planes of your conscious and subconscious mind.

Remember that your hands are empty because your mind is empty. There are no empty hands, just empty minds. Empty, meaning that you are not overflowing with positive thoughts for yourself. Increase your thoughts and you increase the abundance of positive experiences you can imagine. What you put in your mind and allow to stay in your mind. Will determine the fullness of your hands.

On the next page you will find the ten principles to follow to ensure your hands are full and overflowing in an abundance of blessings at all times.

The 10 Principles for Full Hands

These ten principles will keep your hands full and keep you living the No Empty Hands lifestyle.

1. I will not approach anyone with empty hands, as I would not like empty hands to be approached on me.

2. If it is not of value, just leave it where it is. Who wants to collect a bunch of nothing? Seriously.

3. Trust your instincts and think for yourself. If you cannot do it for yourself then who can? The mind can achieve anything it can conceive.

4. You will always keep full hands. Full hands mean, keeping your mind full of the right positive thinking, you can only be a blessing with full hands.

5. Have self-love and abundance first, it all starts with you. You are the beginning of any situation you will find yourself in.

6. Always be real with yourself, if you cannot be real with yourself who can you be real with? You cannot do for others what you cannot do for yourself first.

7. You are only responsible for minding your business *(cultivating your mind to think positive thoughts of desire)* keeping your own hands full. You cannot make it your business to fill anyone's hands but your own.

8. Protect your energy *(emotions)* from empty handed situations.

9. Your hands are as empty as your mind. If a full mind equals full hands, and your hands are empty. The question to answer then is, what are you thinking about?

10. Greet everyone you meet with a blessing, put everything you learned from this guide into action to work through any empty-handed situation.

Chapter Six

Meditation and Affirmations

To meditate is to sit quietly with yourself and collapse time and space in your mind. When you do this, you align your thoughts to the frequency to attract your desire in the physical world. I tend to meditate in the morning and at night before sleeping. Doing this daily to motivate yourself is the best way to get to know yourself. Meditation helps you to focus on yourself and think about the things that make you feel good

When you meditate you are bringing your conscious awareness of being in harmony with the subconscious reality of cause. This is the only way to turn thoughts into things. Meditating allows the subconscious to beware of what you are aware of being by your thoughts. This awareness is expressed as I AM. You cannot separate your I AM from that which you think you are. When you say I AM your subconscious causes manifestation of that, you are aware of being. Knowing this it is important to shut out negative thoughts and focus on positive expressions of thought. Meditating allows you to feel your thoughts in your mind.

Remember nothing happens without feeling.

One the next page you will find steps to the basics of meditation.

Steps to Meditation

Meditate every day, start with just 5 to 10 mins up to 30 mins or more. Please do what is best for you.

1. Choose a quiet spot

2. Relax and close your eyes

3. Take deep breaths in and out. Breathing in positive intentions and breathing out thoughts and negative feelings with each.

4. Focus your mind on something or nothing at all

5. Stay in this state and feel the energy within you.

6. End in a state of gratitude of thanks

The difference between Meditation and Affirmation is that; meditation is when you are inwardly focusing on your awareness with your mind and affirmation is when you are focusing your awareness outwardly giving your thoughts physical expressions through speaking even before it physically has manifested.

On the next pages, are my favorite affirmations to recite to put my mind in alignment with the thoughts that I desired. Affirmations breath life info thoughts which become actual physical thing.

Say these affirmations aloud to yourself throughout the day for 7 days up to 30 days until you can feel every word as true.

Affirmation #1

There is Power and Energy guiding my day.

There is no one to impress and nothing to compete for.

I need to do nothing but believe in, trust, and know this to be true.

There is more than enough good for all who seek it. I AM blessed and I am a blessing.

All is well.

Affirmation #2

In my world, magic and miracles are happening daily.

I find beauty in the simple and luxury things of life.

I expect life to go well today because my world is formed by my thoughts.

My world is a place of clear skies and sunshine.

The magic is in me because I see with spiritual vision and not physical sight alone.

I am grateful, alert, and ready to accept all the gifts of the universe today.

Affirmation # 3

I greet this day with peace and love.

I give only my full attention to the good I desire.

My mind's focused on appreciation and gratitude.

I am enjoying myself now and happy to see what is next.

Affirmation #4

Love is possible.

The universe creates me as love and there is no need to seek for what I already am.

I let go of all defenses that used to guard my heart.

I am open, vulnerable, and available for love in all its forms.

I am loving, loved and lovable.

Affirmation #5

I ask not for riches but for wisdom in using the gift that I received at birth, the ability to control my own mind and use it to attain anything I desire.

I am happy, I am rich, I am healthy, I am grateful.

All things are possible to the one who believes.

This moment is enough, and I am enough for this moment

I AM Happy Bonus Affirmation #1

I am happy because I feel happy.

I only want to do things and hear things that feels happy to me.

I want to be around people that are happy, and I want to be in places that are happy for me.

I feel happy when I do the things I want to do, and I go to the places I want to go.

I am happy because I AM. I have a happy positive outlook for my life.

I AM Money Bonus Affirmation #2

I love money, and money loves me.

Money is made for me to use for my good.

Investing money feels good to me.

Having money to use as I want feels good to me.

I love having money in all my accounts available to me whenever I want it.

I only accept positive and beneficial use of money.

I am grateful to have the use of money whenever I want it.

I AM
Successful Bonus
Affirmation #3

I am successful and everything is happening for my good.

The pay for the work I am doing is equal to the effort I give to earn it.

The effort I give is equal to the amount of success I think I deserve.

I deserve to be paid for the effort I am giving to be successful.

I give quality service and effort in return for the rewards of all the success I desire.

I want to become well known for what I love to do.

I AM Healthy
Bonus
Affirmation #4

I am healthy and my body feels healthy to me.

My mind is free from worry and my body is free from disease.

My body and mind are working together in perfect harmony.

I live a healthy lifestyle with good exercise and eating habits.

I feel healthy and good.

Write Your Own Affirmations

Use this template to write your own positive phrases of desire.

Use this template to write your own positive phrases of desire.

Chapter Seven

12 Mind Energies to Keep You Motivated

To reach even higher levels of *I Don't Give A D*MN*. There are the twelve energies of the mind you will need to discipline and take control of to keep yourself motivated. How they are expressed in your life is up to you to gain control of. Leaving these energies uncontrolled will leave you subjected to them working against you and undoing what you work hard to accomplish. Left uncontrolled, these energies will allow every negative thought to take on the form of negative emotions and negative experiences in your life. All chaos and confusion in your life is linked to how you use these energies of the mind.

These energies represent the nature of your thoughts and how you express them. When you have complete control of these energies you will be tapping into the creative power of the universe at will, to have anything you want, anytime you want it. You will be able to do things others say or think are impossible. Your mind will serve you, only the good things in life as you want them. These are the twelve energies of the mind, given to you as the foundation of your mind's ability to create the world you desire it to be.

Focus these energies on only the important things. It is quite common for people to focus their energy on things that are not important. When your emotional energy is spent on things that are not important it can be very draining. The first thing you need to do is to be noticeably clear about the things in your life that are important to you. This way, things will not bother you so much. And you will know when something really is worth the energy or not. In most cases you will find that you are wasting energy and letting certain circumstances and things bother you that you should not. This can be unhealthy and cause you to block your own blessing. When you are clear about the important things. You will maintain a positive attitude and will be happier with your life.

LOVE

The first energy is Love. This energy allows you to control the emotions you express about the things you want. You will be able to respond to challenges in a positive way.

This energy when expressed in a positive way can eliminate any stress or anxieties. With love your possibilities are endless.

However, when this energy is out of control, you express it in a negative way that can keep you full of hate and ungratefulness.

SELF-ESTEEM

The second energy of the mind is related to Self-Esteem. This energy, when disciplined, only permits the good to enter your mind. To only allow good thoughts to impress on your consciousness. No matter what others suggest you believe; you only believe what is going to be in harmony with your defined desire.

Because with time these impressions will become expressions. You will be unmovable to any negative thoughts about you or negative situations happening around you. Your mind will then listen to the commands that only you give it.

It is this energy of your mind that affirms that you are the creator of your circumstances by the things you hear or allow to enter your mind of thought. This energy is the foundation of building faith.

WISDOM

The third energy of the mind is Wisdom or your ability to judge rightly. When you control this energy.

You will be able to react to things with love and positivity, you will be a wise judge in expressing what you want to be as you are conscious of being.

You will know who you are and will be able to let others be as they are without condemnation or criticism.

COURAGE

The fourth energy of the mind is Courage. This energy gives you the ability to appropriate the desire you want despite having any evidence of the desire.

Remaining faithful in the thought and waiting patiently for the unseen to become apparent and realized.

Courage is the energy that will give you the ability to remain faithful that your desire will happen even if the world says it is impossible.

With courage you will know when to act, when to speak up and when to remain silent.

STRENGTH

The fifth energy of the mind is Strength. This energy when controlled gives you the ability to remain uninfluenced by the senses of appearance.

You will be able to stand firm on your beliefs no matter what anyone else thinks about them or you.

You will have completely mastered the freedom of choice.

IMAGINATION

The sixth energy is Imagination. This energy allows you to shine in the darkness of negativity. You will be able to separate your individual ideas of self from the mass ideas of the world.

People like artists, scientists, inventors have vivid imaginations. They often can see well beyond everyone else around them.

Lack of imagination is why most people fail today. They cannot see themselves beyond what they are and where they are now.

It is imagination that can make you a leader and the lack of it can make you a follower. Imagination brings the best out of you and lifts you beyond the limitations of life.

UNDERSTANDING

The seventh energy is Understanding. Understanding will help you work in harmony with others and remove doubt in yourself from your mind.

Understanding will protect you from receiving any unwanted experiences.

You will be able to remain indifferent to what others are saying and doing, that is not in harmony with what you desire to express.

SELF-CONTROL

The eighth energy is Self-Control. This energy gives power to self-expression.

When controlled, you will be able to express yourself positively no matter the situation.

You will master your thoughts and your expressions of thoughts will be expressed positively. Only you can control yourself.

JUDGEMENT

The ninth energy of the mind is Judgement. A clear and ordered mind is required to control this energy.

This energy perceives that which is not revealed to the physical eye of sight. This energy will give you the ability to keep your mind still and not judge from appearances.

This aspect of the mind has the capacity to interpret the good in that you see. It will protect you from being robbed of your positive energy.

GRATITUDE

The tenth energy is Gratitude. With this mind energy, you give thanks for the things that you do not have possession of yet.

Which will in turn open the gates of your imagination. To permit gifts beyond your capacity to receive, be poured over into you.

The amount of gratitude you have for something is how it shows up in your real life experience. The greater the gratitude the greater abundance you will receive of the things you want.

Gratitude + Attitude= thanks giving to turn the unseen into the seen.

JOY

The eleventh energy is Joy. This energy of the mind is controlled when you become conscious of the abundance of life.

You express joy and are happy with where you are and who you are aware of being in the present moment.

No one will be able to steal your joy.

DETACHMENT

The twelfth and last of the energies of the mind is Detachment. This energy of mind will allow you to detach from all things that keep you from becoming the person you want to be and doing the things you want to do.

This energy will give you the strength to let go. You will detach yourself from problems or limitations and place it on the solution. You assume the consciousness of that which you desire to be.

Intro to Journaling

Writing is an extremely healthy way to get to know you. You might want to try writing in a journal or making use of lists. Lists can be immensely helpful for becoming positive and getting to know you. Use this temple journal. Feel motivated to design a life full of positive things that make you happy.

Definitions

i. Affirmations: positive phrases of desire

ii. State: physical conscious awareness of self

iii. Acting: using your imagination

iv. **Atmosphere:** energy

v. **Belief:** living in the assumption of the thought

vi. **By heart**: feeling it

vii. **Conscious:** you as I AM or your awareness of being

viii. **Desire:** ask and it shall be given to you

ix. **Expect:** have faith in or feel

x. **Faith:** living in the assumption of being the thought

xi. **Fear:** doubt in action or worry

xii. **Hope:** belief

xiii. **Minding your business**: cultivating your mind to think positive thoughts of desire

Acknowledgements

I have been blessed to learn from the great expert teachers like Neville Goddard, Napoleon Hill, Abraham Hicks, and Frederick J. Eikerenkoetter II, better known as Reverend Ike. I first learned these teachings on YouTube and then got their books, recordings, and tapes.

For the past 5 years I have been studying and learning about myself. I wrote this guidebook to give you a slight shortcut on compiling the most relevant methods to attaining whatever your heart desires.

I want to thank these teachers and those who made their works accessible for me to examine and make use of. I hope the same will be done with this guide for years to come. I give much LOVE and thank you to all who inspire me to stay motivated to living free.

Reading Book List & Bibliography

1. Think and Grow Rich, written by Napoleon Hill

2. The Power of the Spoken Word, written by Florence Scovel Shinn

3. The Power of Awareness, written by Neville Goddard

4. 12 Disciplines of the mind, audio tape by Reverend Ike Church of the Science of Living.

5. Five steps to alignment, written by Abram Hicks

6. Leading the Field, by Earl Nightingale

7. The Subtle Art of Not Giving a F*CK written by Mark Manson

8. Becoming Supernatural. How Common People Are Doing the Uncommon, written by Joe Dispenza

9. The Twelve Disciples, by Neville Goddard

AVONDA ANDERSON has led a wonderful and extraordinary life. She has over 40 years of life experience to share from raising kids; to landing top jobs in corporate America as a working mother; and starting your own business and how to travel the world in style.

She is a serial entrepreneur and knows what it takes to get what you want, when you need it or want it most. AVONDA has participated on empowering discussion panel and other forums. Has, also been featured on several local and international media outlets highlighting her contributions across business industries including creating beauty consumer brands, to business consulting in Tech, Manufacturing, Financial Services and Sports and Entertainment.

Rafaela Azevedo

AVONDA earned a master's degree in Procurement and Acquisition Management and graduated cum lade from Webster University. She has dedicated her life to higher learning in all forms academically, spirituality and metaphysically. She also shares a strong passion for creating equitable possibilities, as a certified professional in Supplier Diversity and Inclusion.

AVONDA has tried and evaluated the principles and methods in this guidebook and was inspired to write it so you can try and evaluate them too.